POETRY FOR THE LEADER INSIDE YOU

A Search and Rescue Mission for the Heart and Soul

by

Dale Biron

BLUE LIGHT PRESS ◆ 1ST WORLD PUBLISHING

1ST WORLD
PUBLISHING

SAN FRANCISCO ◆ FAIRFIELD ◆ DELHI

POETRY FOR THE LEADER INSIDE YOU
Copyright ©2018 by Dale Biron

1ST WORLD LIBRARY
PO Box 2211
Fairfield, Iowa 52556
www.1stworldpublishing.com

BLUE LIGHT PRESS
www.bluelightpress.com
Email: bluelightpress@aol.com

BOOK, COVER DESIGN
Melanie Gendron

AUTHOR PHOTO
Judy Burgio

FIRST EDITION

Library of Congress Control Number: 2017959414

ISBN 9781421837970

PRAISE FOR
POETRY FOR THE LEADER INSIDE YOU
by Dale Biron

"I have been inspired by Dale's work and his poetry for many years. I only wish I had had this book when I was leading a fast growing company through "the treacherous conditions caused by organizational growth, change and transition." I and the company would have been the better for it."

— David Edward,
    former CEO of The Body Shop Inc.

"This is not a book to be read once and put in the bookcase. It is a daily resource for examining leadership and connecting to ourselves in that pursuit. Dale Biron is masterful at using poetry to facilitate this awakening and giving us a guide for ongoing reflection. It will provoke, stimulate, and inspire you every time you read it."

— Susannah Baldwin Ph.D. —Leadership and
    Communications Coach

"I love to read poetry; but I rarely seek them out as a business book. However, I very much enjoyed reading your introduction and I was very curious to read the poems once I read their titles. Now, I'd like to read them all because they were penned especially to help businessmen and women develop the leadership within us. I sensed that these poems will help us get in touch with own inner being which in turn will help us to get in touch with our students'. It is my hope that I they will become a better student of leadership and teacher. I want to use your book to help me mentor the younger generation of future leaders at La Tortilla Factory." Thank you for writing this book.

— Carlos Tamayo, Chairman of the Board of
    La Tortilla Factory

"I loved your intro and can't wait to get a copy of the final book! I think the poetic/story telling approach is a wonderful way of getting your message across."

— Martin E. Plourd, President & CEO of
    Community West Bank and
    Community West Bancshares

"In the tradition of David Whyte, Dale Biron has found his voice in translating the polarized society in which we live into the subtle and often sublime music of poetry to public offerings and to the corporate arena. The quality of Dale's poetry often takes the ordinary experience of daily life into moments of inspiration."

— Ron Tilden, Organization Consultant
    and Musician

"Dale is a wonderful combination of poet, craftsman, and coach and this fine little work puts his insights on sharp display. I was struck and reminded from the first few pages that we are, and most certainly I am, easily made prisoner of the lurid appeal of logic and reason and an all too natural gravitation towards rapid decision-making. Dale reminds us the settling, opening, and slowing influence of a bit of verse, a spot of poetry, or even a selection from an epic poem. This book should find a comfortable home on the shelves of any seeker of insight, inspiration, or just good common sense guidance."

— Kevin Hoffberg, Sr. Consultant, Retired Executive,
    Citizen Farmer

"I truly believe that if I came back to planet Earth a decade from now, I'd find captains of industry throughout our nation quoting Dale Biron during their board meetings and coffee breaks."

— Dr. Peller Marion, Author of
    Crisis Proof Your Career and *Career Tuneup*

DEDICATION

This book is dedicated to Margot Fraser (1929 – 2017), the brilliant, kind and humble founder of Birkenstock, USA. She was a client, mentor and dear friend for over 25 years. Margot was the first leader to encourage me to use the poetry I loved so much in my work with leaders and their teams. Her love for the power of language helped me imagine helping others with the unique and creative tool called poetry.

Abschied und danke mein lieber Freund

A Special Thanks ...

This book has been a dream for years. I owe a deep bow of gratefulness and thanks to so many amazing people who helped me on this path of delight and discovery. That would include dear friends, colleagues and clients alike, as well as hundreds of workshop and class participants. You each gave me the priceless gift of your interest, engagement and presence.

As for my love and best friend, Judy Burgio, who faithfully read every chapter and gave me honest and incredibly helpful feedback, I have no words adequate for my gratitude. And for me, that is saying a lot! You had total faith in me and this project, and you kept saying, *"just do it"*... again and again. I should have taken your advice sooner.

Jo Anne Smith, you've been a dear friend and my gifted editor for this book and other projects. I treasure both roles you have played in my work and life. Wendy Palmer, George Leonard and Richard Heckler with whom I studied Aikido for many years, you never leave my thoughts and feelings for long. Another dear mentor-friend, Brother David Steindl-Rast you taught me how to drag gratefulness into every nook and cranny of my life. To Tom Rusk, M.D. who first introduced me to the power of the universal human and leadership values of *respect, understanding, caring and fairness*, what a gift you gave. Yes, and Alan Watts you taught me to think wildly on my own and take life sincerely and not so seriously.

Thanks to Chief Editor, Diane Frank at Blue Light Press who was deeply supportive throughout the entire process. And thanks also to Melanie Gendron for her distinctive and creative design work.

Let me also acknowledge several other dear friends and colleagues who encouraged this work and whose feedback and ideas made it so much better: Susannah Baldwin, you gave countless hours and so much energy to this humble project. Donna Casella, I am certain that had you not insisted I follow my poetic passion at Dominican University in the OLLI program, I would not be nearly as far along with my work. Richard Berkvam, so delightful and helpful the hours we spent talking about the art of story telling. Ron Tilden, what a sage friend you have been for all these years. Peller Marion, Tom Tolman, Justin Sherman, all of you long-time and dear friends kept your support so strong. Kat Braeman, thanks for your editorial input that was so helpful. Kevin Hoffberg, friend and collegue for many years, your wise comments and help were deeply appreciated. Jay Hamilton-Roth, those long walks and talks were priceless in helping to sort things out. And Kim Stafford, fellow writer and amazing poet, your encouragement over the years has been so helpful and inspirational.

Of course this book features my work with leaders and their teams. There have been more leaders and team members to thank than these few pages could hold, however let me single out just a few senior executives for whom I have the deepest level of respect. They are leading (or have lead) amazing organizations and teams with such grace and skill: David

Edward, David Vogel, Janice Stewart, Marty Plourd, Carlos Tamayo, Steve Herron, Larry Brackett, Joel Goldsmith, Fred Fisher, Juelle Fisher, Rob Fisher, Rick Davis, Ty Pforsich and Charles Moore. I am indebted to and have learned so much from each of you. Lastly, I want to thank my brother Joe Biron who is a fine leader and writer himself, who has championed all my life's greatest passions and projects. Also, thanks to my sister Lucy Lustig Biron who has such a deep and soulful understanding of art and its stunning potential. Some of your wisdom rubbed off on me. And, of course huge thanks to every dear and talented poet who allowed me to use your poems in this modest work of mine. What a gift you have given.

And speaking of poets, I especially want to thank the late William Stafford, the greatest poet who ever lived, who passed from this plane in 1993. You lucky readers will find a number of his poems featured here in these pages. I discovered the work of Bill Stafford just a few years after his death. For many years since then, few days have passed without my reading at least one of his poems or essays. His unique and powerful ideas about reconciliation, writing, living, and leading are infused throughout this book. I wish I could have said this to you in person Bill, the words you used to close so many of your personal communications … *Thanks and Adios!*

With a deep bow of gratefulness, I thank you all!

TABLE OF CONTENTS

Poetry for the Leader Inside You

A Search and Rescue Mission for the Heart and Soul

Put your ear to the wall of your heart.
Listen for the whisper of knowing there.

—— Tom Barrett, Poet

They were smart, capable, courageous climbers, yet both nearly died on that spring night, on a fourteen thousand foot mountain. The weather was beautiful and clear that morning, but they started a little late. As seasoned climbers, they knew what equipment was required, but it was only a day hike so they decided to leave certain emergency and survival items behind. They also knew the ironclad rule of keeping your *turnaround time* sacred, but the summit was so close, so tempting, they kept pushing on a little longer.

Each small mistake, each tiny lapse of judgment, was not enough to cause harm. But all of them together, combined with other circumstances, conspired to create significant injury, pain, and near catastrophe.

When they finally reached the summit, it was well past their estimated time of arrival. By now they had started to worry a little, but still things seemed okay as they prepared to "glissade" down the mountain. (*A controlled slide on your butt in the snow.*) For the first thousand feet, all was good and even fun. But then something went very wrong. Controlled slides by both climbers turned into terror-filled falls down the side of a now severely icy mountain. Both climbers careened out of control, slamming into boulders and rocks, one landing five feet short of an instant death fall. A single foothold kept her on a precarious perch just above the abyss below.

Now seriously injured, hurting, and separated, each afraid the other had already died, there was only one choice … it was imperative that they call for rescue. But now after the fall with a cell phone that must surely be shattered, their prospects dimming, how would making a call be possible?

Fate, luck, or divine intervention, whatever your belief, this is what actually happened.

Thankfully tucked inside a pocket, their cell phone survived the fall and miraculously allowed a call to 911. This began a critical series of events that ultimately saved their lives. The climber's strength, courage, and intelligence combined with the calm, equally courageous persistence of the search and rescue team made the life-saving difference. Which brings us to the point of our story and this small book.

A Different Kind of Search and Rescue
(Especially for Leaders …)

Even the smartest, most capable leaders can have brief lapses of judgment and make their own version of small incremental mistakes. Just as with our climbers, leaders can also miss the subtle signs of challenge and even danger along the way, so easy to do given the fierce pace and pressures of our work lives.

Leaders, like our climbers, can get too attached to getting farther than they need to. For example, when a leader meets an important goal, and then decides to add another on at the end, they can push themselves and their team into a kind of red zone of exhaustion and stress. At these times, leaders and teams, not at their best, are more prone to making relationship-damaging mistakes.

And of course, just like our climbers who left behind several pieces of critical equipment, thinking they were unnecessary for their situation, leaders can make similar mistakes. For example, leaders who do not slow down long enough to reflect and catch up with themselves. They may also neglect to seek the ideas and feedback of others or simply to listen more fully before launching some critical new project.

Also, just as our climbers failed to anticipate how rapidly the snow would freeze over, turning treacherous as soon as the sun began to set, so too leaders can forget the treacherous conditions caused by organizational growth, change and transition. And how much skill, understanding and empathy are called for in such situations.

And finally, like our climbers, these situations for leaders can call for their own unique version of search and rescue, which is just what this book is about. Each *special search and rescue project*, designed for you, the leader, is anchored by a relevant poem, with examples and stories uniquely effective at supporting access to a critical leadership quality. Here the stakes are not literally life and death, but are about the critical life of the heart and soul, which, after all, are the source of our true power and is behind all our personal and business successes.

Why It Works?

First, the poetry we'll feature works by flying underneath the radar screen of our linear strategic minds. No doubt, we need our logical skills to succeed. However, in the domain of the heart and soul, the non-linear, intuitive, and imaginative parts of us hold sway. Therefore, the poetry-based search and rescue tools featured in this book are designed for plumbing the heart and the soul for the critical, universal qualities that are already inside us—qualities that often get obscured, overlooked and forgotten in the rush and crush of our daily lives.

These poems (turned into practical tools) are able to grow and change us, because paradoxically they are *not* trying to do so. The poems have nothing to sell or gain by withholding their truth—each one repurposed here has no mission or intention other than being as truthful and clear as possible.

There is also a growing body of neuroscience research on poetry. While having people engage with poetry in different ways, researchers have looked at everything from brain scans, heart rate, and facial expressions, to the movement of skin and arm hairs (aka, *goose bumps*). It turns out nothing engages us quite like poetry. Interestingly, the chills and goose bumps were reported to have occurred most often at the *"aha"* moments in poems, especially at the end of stanzas and whole poems, where insights and deeper feelings of connection most often occur. My experience supports these findings.

How It Works

How do these poems actually shift our thinking, feelings

and ultimately our actions, helping us rescue our most skillful and empathetic responses? It's actually simpler than you might imagine. The poems that work best for our purposes combine three critical characteristics: they are *short*, *surprising* and *sustaining*.

Short: First, we do not want even an ounce of extra baggage to obscure the images and metaphors featured in the poem. These images help us *get* what needs getting without a need to understand, at least not at first. Our goal then, is economical leanness. Meaning, nothing should get in the way. Meaning, nothing to wade through to get to the core. Truth is, our attention is more easily maintained if the poem is short.

Surprising: Verbs, nouns, adjectives, adverbs, pronouns, etc. We hitch up these common parts of speech in uncommon ways. Normally, we use words and language as utilities and tools to describe the world, provide instructions, and reassure each other that the world is just as we sense and think it is. But the well-selected poem is different. It starts with what we know, then suddenly lifts off into new and unexpected places. Which is to say, we are brought back to a place we know by heart.

Sustaining: Once the new images and metaphors gain our attention and enter our awareness, and the surprise has opened us up to what is right here, right now, we are left with a feeling of *yes*, this works. It is a kind of sustenance that empowers, feeds and sustains us deeply. It facilitates and allows us to have our own unique experience and way of *seeing* the world, bringing us back to our true power. It is a feeling that rescues us from the stress and difficulty that is always waiting in the wings of our post-modern world, but need not pull us down.

For Example

In Chapter 1, we'll confront the quality of courage head-on. It features one of the most *wallet-requested poems* I've used with leaders, their teams and workshop participants. I say the poem confronts courage head-on because it's unflinching in telling the truth (as seen by the poem) regarding our life's purpose. One leader loved this poem so much he immediately asked for a copy. He said reading it was like getting a *chiropractic adjustment for the soul.*

We'll get to that chapter soon, but first here are a few more thoughts about why poems make good and effective search and rescue teams for the qualities underneath our best actions as leaders—qualities like integrity, resilience and wisdom.

Let me illustrate with the words of leaders and workshop participants themselves. I have a rich history of working with leaders who've used these poems and others, telling me exactly why and how they felt supported. Here are a few sample comments from over the years:

- *After hearing this poem, I felt a deep sense of excitement for who I was when I first started my company. I haven't felt that way for years.*
- *You realize as a leader that some decisions you make, no matter which way you decide, have no upside. It is freeing, however, to name the elephant in the room.*
- *"I felt a keen sense of satisfaction and belonging to something bigger than myself."*
- *"The question that poem asked about kindness will forever haunt me … in a good way."*
- *"All I can say is I give my people too much advice. I'm going to stop doing that."*

> • *"I always thought confusion should be avoided at all cost. Now I see it's my secret weapon for innovation and creativity."*

This Book Is For You If You Feel That ...

1. Leaders (veteran and emerging) need nothing added from the outside. You already have a reservoir of universal leadership qualities inside you. These qualities are you, so the critical place to search for them is inside not out.

2. Access to these natural qualities, and therefore to success, will depend on your awareness, perspective, and the context you create for yourself.

3. At any given time, the level of your stress, challenge and discouragement will conspire to close-off access to your success-sustaining qualities.

4. Opening the critical conduit to these qualities is not about force, control, or even effort—rather it's about listening, remembering, and letting be.

Why This Book May (Not) Be For You

As leaders, we have come to expect instant, ready-made rules—lists and formulas offered to us as the answer to all our leadership challenges. Famous leaders are served up as *models* for us to emulate. I know it's meant to be helpful, and no doubt it can be. Who among us cannot learn valuable lessons from leaders like Abraham Lincoln, Eleanor Roosevelt, or Martin Luther King, Jr.?

I simply resist the notion that we can copy our way to great leadership. My experience is that such ideas are naïve at best, and damaging at worse.

The path to your success is uniquely yours to define and live. And that path is one shoulder wide. Your success as a leader will come from inside you, and good poems have unique ways to reveal what is there. As a coach, I constantly work at providing support without constraint, as well as ideas, questions and encouragement without preachiness, but my approach is not for everyone.

It's likely as you use this book and encounter different poems, you'll find yourself saying things like, *"Wait a minute. That poem didn't work for me. Or that poem might have something to say about empathy as suggested, but what it's really about is respect or wisdom or _____?"* If this doesn't happen, I've not done my job. No one has a *pipeline to the truth* when it comes to you, leadership, or poetry. A consistently helpful trait of good poems used as search and rescue teams, is they invite each of us to walk *inside the poems* and have our own unique experience.

Everyone Leads and Everyone Who Leads ... Gets Stuck

This book is not simply for traditional leaders. It's for emerging leaders as well, who are wisely practicing on themselves before attempting to lead others. This book is also for leaders who get stuck, which means of course all leaders. All leaders get stuck at times in old patterns and habits. This is another way of saying we get stuck by not fully tapping into and harnessing the authentic, natural qualities inside us.

Rest assured, as you read this book, all the parts of you will be honored, supported, and respected. Yes, even the stuck parts. Maybe especially those parts.

You'll find in the pages ahead, leaders, team members, and workshop participants who are seekers and learners, engaged with every bump, challenge, and triumph along the way. Some I've known for years, others I've met more recently. I care about each one of them. They are all courageous, brilliant and skilled leaders.

You will meet them through their stories and comments. But most of all, you will meet them through the poems they have selected, loved, continue to love, and use on an ongoing basis. These poems were chosen to serve them as dynamic tools, yes and as search and recue teams for the heart and soul, whenever they felt the need to conduct their own just-in-time missions to find and recover the qualities of their best selves. The amazing life and leadership qualities they had all along … just like you.

One Last Word of Encouragement for Your *Inner Skeptic*

I can imagine what you might be saying right now. *"OK Dale, I may already have inside me all the qualities your book describes, just waiting to be invoked more often and more fully. However, at times I feel a kind of low ink condition for certain of these qualities. So if I have them, some may occasionally exist in rather small quantities."*

Of course! I understand. It's true for every person I've ever met, known, or coached. And it doesn't matter how talented or successful. The point is this. Great poems (like great stories) bring both covert and overt powers to the game. All we need is an ounce, a drop or even a dried up speck of a particular quality. Any amount will do as a starting point for moving forward.

Poems that engage and move us are amazingly potent tools. Like wise Shamans, they're able to shape shift something out of almost nothing. Drop them down inside you and simply let them do their work. Once you begin to cultivate even a smidgen of an internal quality, it begins to grow and expand. I have seen this over and over. So even on days when you feel none, these poems *(and others)* can help you create *some*.

Lastly, the best news is that once you get started on this journey, you'll begin to find your own poems to support you in ways you haven't yet imagined. *(They are all around you once you start looking.)* Suddenly you will have a whole new set of *just-in-time* tools to help you navigate your own unique path and to help you help others along their path of learning, growth, and success. After all, isn't that the whole point of being a good leader?

CHAPTERS

1. The Girl Who Dreamed Too Big (Courage: The Way It Is By William Safford)

2. The Seductive Power of Being Right (Mindfulness: The Place Where We Are Right By Yehuda Amichai / Translated by Chana Bloch and Stephen Mitchell)

3. What Your People Really Want (Staying True: The Contract By William Ayot)

4. A Betrayal in the Mind (Understanding: A Ritual To Read to Each Other By William Stafford)

5. Why Gratefulness Matters Hugely for Leaders (Gratitude: Gratefulness by Dale Biron)

6. A Beautiful Baffled Mind (Humility: The Real Work by Wendell Berry)

7. How to Make Frightening Requests (of Ourselves) (Boldness: SOMETIMES By David Whyte)

8. How to Be a Person (Integrity: Being A Person By William Stafford)

9. When to Let Your Heart Decide (Resilience: Decisions by Dale Biron)

10. Why Only Kindness Makes Sense (Caring: Kindness By Naomi Shihab Nye)

11. Leading Between the Rocks and Hard Places (Wisdom: Traveling Through The Dark By William Stafford)

12. The Perfect Way to Procrastinate (Productivity: Ode To Procrastination By Dale Biron)

13. The Trouble with Hero-Leaders (Empowerment: It's heavy to drag, this big sack By William Stafford)

14. How to Be an Emotionally Intelligent Leader (Empathy: May By Bruce Weigl)

15. Are We Really on Our Own Side? (Happiness: Sun Trail By Dale Biron)

16. How Much Is Enough? (Fairness: The Moral Dilemma of Yellow By Dale Biron)

The Girl Who Dreamed Too Big

"For me, poetry is always a search for order."
— Elizabeth Jennings

In all my years as a leadership coach and business consultant, I had never met anyone like her. She had a unique combination of passion, humility, courage and curiosity, plus a deep commitment to her vision of what a business could *stand for* and *be*.

Margot had what John Keats called *negative capacity*, which means she was able to tolerate and even thrive with a far greater degree of uncertainty, doubt and mystery than most leaders can tolerate. This allowed the discovery of new, more creative ways to accomplish critical goals. And it allowed her to give others the space to grow, learn and accomplish their own goals.

To my delight, Margot gave early validation to my own experience that the powerful language of poetry could provide practical guidance and strength for a leader. Yes, I mean effective *search and rescue missions* for the heart and soul.

She was never a traditional executive, the kind seen triumphantly beaming from the cover of a glitzy business magazine. And yet, she built from scratch one of the most successful, iconic, groundbreaking companies in American business history. The company was Birkenstock USA. The leader was Margot Fraser.

The first time we met in the mid '90s, we of course talked about leadership and coaching. But that wasn't all. To my delight, we also talked about poetry and, more specifically, the great German poet Rilke. It was more than 20 years ago, early in my coaching career, and I had just started using poetry in my work. When I mentioned my interest in poetry, she smiled and told me that poetry had saved her life as a teenager growing up in war-ravaged Germany.

Expectantly, I moved to the edge of my chair, readying myself for the story to follow. Margot was born the year of the great worldwide economic crash of 1929. She grew up with anti-Nazi parents trapped inside their native Germany. From the moment WW II started, Margot and her family were thrust into danger. Internal danger from the ever-present menace of the Nazi Party and external danger from the constant bombings of Berlin by the Allied forces.

Margot once told me that during those dark times something as innocent as a school essay describing a forbidden comment or action, fallen into the wrong hands, could spell disaster. Even the slightest hint of disloyalty or defiance could place a person or whole family in serious jeopardy.

Here's a brief excerpt describing those years, from a book co-authored by Margot entitled *Dealing with the Tough Stuff—Practical Wisdom for Running a Values-Driven Business.*

> *I grew up in Berlin during the war. The principal of my elementary school was an old Prussian lady—anti-Nazi like my parents—and she instilled in me the belief that girls were capable of anything and should follow their dreams. During my last year of school, the city was already very*

damaged by bombs, but the school still offered counseling for
children about their careers. Though I hadn't told anyone,
I already knew I wanted to go into business.

And dream she did. In fact, the core thread of Margot's
life was determined in those early teenage years. She told
her father she wanted to show the world a different side of
Germany. She would show a peaceful and productive side,
following in the spirit and tradition of the great German
merchant traders, who had captured her heart and mind
in her favorite books.

However, the traders were all men. So, while Margot's
father was loving and supportive, he feared her dreams
were simply too big and grand for a woman of her times.
He feared she was setting herself up to be deeply disap-
pointed. But Margot was not just any young girl. From
that point in her life on, Margot would continue to defy
expectations, meet challenges, scale walls and break glass
ceilings. She once told me it might have been good that
she didn't go to business school, where they likely would
have taught that her dreams were impossible!

And speaking of *the impossible*, she rarely let that get in her
way. In fact, once Margot took possession of those first
few pairs of Birkenstock shoes, she became undaunted in
her mission.

At first, she faced constant rejection. The shoes were com-
fortable and healthy, but looked so strange. These were
shoes that only a few counterculture health food stores
would reluctantly agree to stock. But that didn't last. After
those early years, Birkenstock shoes would transform into
an American cultural icon, earning a permanent place in
the imaginations of millions.

Meanwhile, back to the Germany of Margot's youth, the war continued to drag on as life in Berlin deteriorated. Every day brought a new level of destruction, until Margot and her family were forced to escape the city, just barely, with little more than their lives. Margot had studied dress-making and used her talents to keep her family alive while exiled in the countryside.

Of course, by that time the German currency had collapsed, and they were now faced with a barter system. She was able to trade eggs, butter and other staples for clothing she made for the farmers' families.

My point in telling this story is twofold. First is being inspired by an ordinary woman who did extraordinary things. Second is to highlight this unique tool for leaders called poetry. One leader I worked with declared poetry to be the original, full-strength *reframing tool*. Of course, how we perceive and *frame* the world has everything to do with how we *experience and succeed* in that world.

For Margot, it was poetry, even during the darkest days of the war, that nurtured and kept her *spirits* and *inner life* alive. And much later, it was poetry that helped *(and often rescued)* her through many business challenges as well.

Throughout the years I worked with Margot at Birken-stock, we continued to talk about poetry right along side the ongoing challenges and opportunities of the business. Margot and I talked about poetry's practical role in both our business and personal lives. One of the poems she appreci-ated very much was by William Stafford. It's a poem about the essential, straightforward and even fierce truths about living in the world. It talks about the essential *thread* of our lives, making it a perfect search and rescue tool for leaders.

The Way It Is

There's a thread you follow. It goes among
things that change. But it doesn't change.
People wonder about what you are pursuing.
You have to explain about the thread.
But it is hard for others to see.
While you hold it you can't get lost.
Tragedies happen; people get hurt
or die; and you suffer and get old.
Nothing you do can stop time's unfolding.
You don't ever let go of the thread.
— William Stafford

In addition to Margot, many leaders over the years have felt this poem was written *just* for them. In fact, so many have asked for copies, that it's become one of my top *wallet-requested poems*. No doubt in Margot's case, many people in her life *wondered about what she was pursuing*. For example, those storeowners where Margot first tried to sell her odd-looking shoes didn't really understand what she was up to, at least not in the beginning.

Of course, no matter how hard it was *for others to see*, she did not waver. And just as the poem promises, by holding tight to her *thread*, Margot did not get lost. Or if she did on occasion, she did not stay lost. Rather, she turned sore feet and backs into healthy, comfortable feet and backs. And well beyond that, Margot touched the hearts and souls of thousands who came in contact with her through her work and life. She did that by staying deeply connected to her own heart and soul.

Also, just as this Stafford poem does not shy away from the fierce realities of life, Margot (and many other leaders

I've worked with) never romanticized business. Despite her unprecedented success, especially as a woman leader and entrepreneur, she knew there were plenty of difficulties, conundrums and problems that had to be faced. In fact, Margot once said that her experience in the war taught her that you *never really own anything—everything in life is only on loan.*

The poetry Margot loved reflected back to her a world of creativity, possibility and hope. Of course these were the qualities she most needed during those harrowing years of war, years that were so often filled with destruction, fear and hopelessness.

An Unspoken Thread

There was another thread that also ran through Margot's life. I never heard her speak of it directly, but there is little doubt she lived it deeply. That thread was ... love. Actually it was two kinds of love.

The first kind is the love for the vision and the service provided in pursuit of that vision. Margot fell in love with Birkenstock shoes in 1966. She was visiting a health spa in her native Germany, when to her own great surprise and delight, she found shoes that actually made her feet and back feel wonderful. Having had troubles for years with her back and feet, the relief was immediate, intense and yes, inspiring. She wanted to pass that love and healing relief along to others.

The second kind of love is the love for the people who are attracted to join the determined effort to make the vision come true. Leaders demonstrate that love by showing people they *belong*, and by embodying the universal values of *respect, understanding, caring and fairness.* Margot was the poster-child for this second kind of love as well. And I can tell you first hand that people joined Margot's vision, dreams and company by the hundreds. I know. I had the pleasure of working with many of them.

Are there portable principles for all of us here? Yes, because every skilled leader I've ever worked with or observed from afar, modeled some version of these two loves.

As leaders, you and I can do the same.

I can tell you this, that young German girl so many years ago, in the middle of such devastating circumstances, who fell in love with poetry and with becoming a great merchant, made an indelible mark on both the world and so many of its inhabitants' hearts. And because she, an ordinary person, dreamed so big and bold, we can too.

Finally, there is one other piece to this story. As I finish this chapter and soon this book, I am also preparing to attend a memorial celebration of Margot's life. For the world has lost a good and wise human being.

In fact, as a dear friend recently told me, some souls seem to leave especially large gaps when they first depart this physical plane. But then later, their spirit grows even larger and more present in our lives.

Margot will be grieved and missed by many, and yet I'm certain that over time, her spirit will grow to even greater proportions within the minds, hearts and lives of those she has touched and will touch through her legacy in the coming years.

Again, why tell this story? It is to remind us all what's at stake and what is possible. It's to show the power of poetry as a practical tool to explore, understand and support our interior lives both at work and home. And finally, to show how an ordinary woman accomplished so many extraordinary things by holding firmly to her life's core thread.

Questions for Your Journal

One main theme of this chapter is courage, the courage to name and follow your own thread. I invite you to answer and journal about any of the following questions that you find interesting, helpful and engaging.

1. Is their value in knowing your *thread*?

2. What is the thread of your own work and life?

3. What vision is it leading you toward?

4. How are people served by you pursuing this vision?

5. How do you explain your thread to others?

6. What difficulty have you encountered explaining or following your thread?

7. Where might you need to *"let go"* and where might you need to *"get going"*?

8. What conspires to make you lose the feel and guidance of your thread?

9. What do you do to reconnect with and follow your thread?

10. How else might you use this poem?

11. Where might you find other poems to help you be more courageous?

12. What must you do, say and remember right now …
to be your best self?

Your Life's Thread Exercise
(Especially for you visual learners.)

Label the significant events in your life in each of the small
circles. In the larger circle, imagine and describe the thread
that ties all the events together. Add more small circles as
needed. Replicate for additional threads. Journal about
what you learn. Journal any changes in your life and in
your leadership you feel are needed.

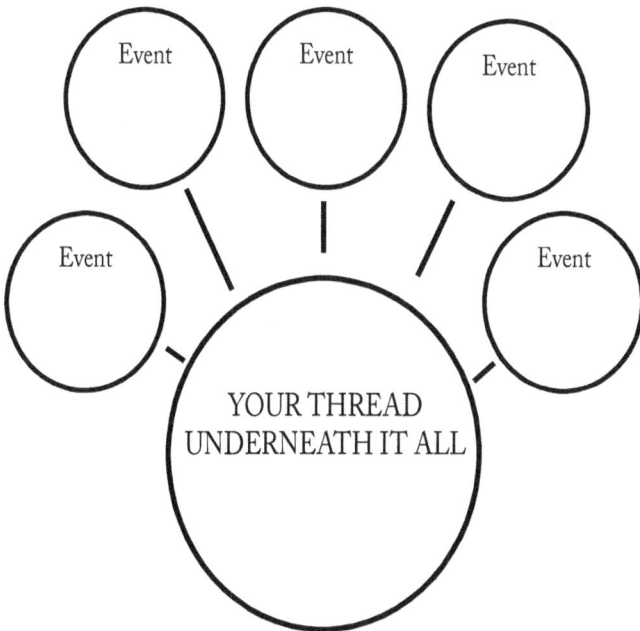

The Seductive Power of Being Right

*"I have many faults, but being wrong
ain't one of them."*

— Jimmy Hoffa

You could feel the tension. Eyes meeting across the conference table spoke volumes. Yes, there were words, but they were drowned out by the visceral communication of voice tone, inflection and body language. It all said, *"I am right ... end of discussion."*

This *"being right"* stance is alive and well in both our business and personal lives. Even when applied in more subdued and subtle ways, the effect is the same. It damages trust, transparency and, ultimately, relationships. I remember in particular, preparing for a retreat by interviewing every team member who worked for a senior executive coaching client. Several team members reported that this leader cared more about *being right* than anything else. Yes, including success.

Of all the challenges for which I've coached leaders, an *excessive need to be right* is one of the most typical and most damaging. It's at the core of the majority of our communication and interpersonal challenges at work and, of course, in our personal lives as well.

But the problem goes deeper.

Our need to be right doesn't just damage relationships and productivity, though that is plenty to worry about. This need also damages our ability to avoid problems in the first place, and once they do occur, it dramatically and negatively impacts our ability to solve them.

Why is this the case? Because, we often don't even see our most difficult challenges as they barrel down the highway toward us. We get so focused, and yes stuck, on our own rock-solid position and point of view, that we're unable to respond to or even see actual circumstances and events happening right before our eyes.

But before we go further, let me introduce the poem reserved for this chapter. And like the other poems in this book, I've used this one many times with various leaders, team members, audiences and in my own life.

The Place Where We Are Right

From the place where we are right
Flowers will never grow
In the spring.

The place where we are right
Is hard and trampled
Like a yard.

But doubts and loves
Dig up the world
Like a mole, a plow.
And a whisper
will be heard in the place
Where the ruined
House once stood.

> — **Yehuda Amichai** Translated by Chana Bloch
>   and Stephen Mitchell

What do you think? Does the poem resonate with you? Let me add some additional lines, which for me summarize the impact of this poem. These lines are not from this translation, but are attributed to comments made in a presentation by the amazing poet, Robert Bly. The lines are:

It is our certainties that crucify
Our doubts and our loves
Dig up the world
And the flowers can then grow.

When I use this poem at workshops and in presentations, just mentioning the title invariably gets a chuckle. We laugh, because we *get it*. We laugh because this poem nails us at one of the places in our psyches where we have the least clarity and yet, the most vulnerability. This is why this poem makes such a great search and rescue tool for our hearts and souls. Said another way, it helps us recover our mindfulness and sense of belonging to our selves and to the world, just by admitting we may not *(always)* be right.

Both science and common sense demonstrate how we humans are naturally biased toward confirming our existing ideas and convictions. The phenomenon has a name. It's called our confirmation bias. It means we actually see and experience a world we expect and believe to be true. We each have a set of core beliefs that we accept as the truth. It's these mostly unconscious biases that we use to filter the world we see and experience.

This fact has given rise to countless revealing and wise observations. One of my favorites is by Anaïs Nin who said, "We don't see the world as it is, we see it as we are." This is not a bug in our wiring as humans, but rather a prominent feature.

Look at it this way. Do any of us imagine our beliefs perfectly reflect reality? "Of course not," we say! It would be absurd to answer any other way. Even the most aware and observant among us has blind spots. But if our expectations do not perfectly reflect reality, then how exactly will we know which of our beliefs are false and which are true? It's possible but not easy to discern the difference and the Yehuda Amichai poem above provides us a possible roadmap.

At its core, the poem wisely reminds and advises us to hold our beliefs, opinions, and especially our certainties, more lightly. In practical every day terms, we can simply begin to look for, and actually note any evidence that is contrary to our beliefs. Over time, we can break through our unconscious patterns of confirmation bias, making a case for shifting some of our beliefs.

This is a very powerful technique and process for uncovering beliefs that are no longer serving us. This practice allows us to hold our beliefs lightly enough that when the world presents contrary evidence, we'll actually be able to see it. And if we can slow down and see it, maybe we'll have a chance to do something different before a challenge or even a catastrophe strikes.

A happy side effect of using this poem and practice is that our adaptability and creativity can't help but increase. After all, rigid beliefs (aka, being absolutely certain) kill creativity and adaptability like nothing else.

Lets put it this way. One of my favorite sayings is, "don't believe everything you think, just because you think it." But let's be clear about what we are saying here. The fact that we can't believe everything we think does not mean we should not believe anything we think.

This poem reminds us we're in the business of seeking, rather than always knowing the truth. When we keep the open mind of a seeker, we're able to respond moment to moment to the world and to others in the world with grace and skill. In this way, we don't force the truth where it's not, but rather seek the truth where it is.

Does this mean we shouldn't have solid principles and values we hold dear? No, of course not. But, for example, when we hold our truth more lightly, we are able to honor the universal values of respect, understanding, caring and fairness with much greater skill.

There is one more thing to consider. Over time, as a culture we've come to believe that being wrong is the same as being dumb, ill-intended or a "loser." By the time we're adults we take things even farther. By then, we believe mistakes don't simply mean we've done something wrong, but rather that we ourselves are wrong. This attitude kills our confidence, creativity, and ultimately our performance.

Eventually, caught up in the never wrong, perfectionist mode, we stop being able to entertain the possibility or even imagine being wrong. It's at this point we become truly vulnerable and at risk. This is when we are ripe for making huge mistakes and backing our selves into dangerous corners. Remember: It is our certainties that crucify / Our doubts and our loves / Dig up the world / And the flowers can then grow.

Truth is, being right is so deeply embedded into our cultural assumptions that we can scarcely perceive or see it any more. This is why we need great poems and other tools to help remind us what St. Augustine said 1200 years before Descartes, "Fallor ergo sum" which means, "I make mistakes, therefore I am."

What's at Stake?

Taking this poem and its insights to heart will bring many benefits. Perhaps because being right comes so naturally to us all, mindfulness might be the real leadership quality we are highlighting here. Isaac Asimov put it this way, "The saddest aspect of life right now is that science gathers knowledge faster than society gathers wisdom."

Perhaps this is true of leaders as well. Perhaps as leaders, we gather the knowledge to manage faster than we gather the wisdom to lead. And nowhere is this wisdom needed more than to hold our proverbial horses when it comes to always being perfectly certain we are absolutely right.

Questions for Your Journal

The willingness to confront our need to be right requires a kind of steadfast mindfulness. It requires us to stop ourselves in midstream and consider other people, ways of seeing, ways of being and doing things. I invite you to answer and journal any of the following questions that you find interesting, helpful and engaging.

1. What does being right mean to you?

2. What does being wrong say about you?

3. What circumstances create an excessive need to be right for you?

4. Describe the last time you had an argument about being right?

5. Can you learn to love and appreciate your flaws and mistakes as much as your ideas and insights?

6. Can you hold your beliefs just a little lighter, thereby modeling that for others that look to you for leadership?

7. How can you put this poem to work for you?

What Your People Really Want

"Be true to yourself. Make each day a masterpiece."
— John Wooden

Of course, people work for traditional reasons, not the least of which is earning money to manage their livelihood. But there are deeper motivations that are harder to describe, yet that matter to all of us in our work lives and shape what we seek and expect from our leaders.

So what is it that your people really want from you, their leader? Let's look at how one insightful and accomplished poet has answered the question.

Contract—A Word from the Led

And in the end we follow them —
not because we are paid,
not because we can see some advantage,
not because of what they have accomplished,
not even because of the dreams they dream,
but simply because of who they are:
the man, the woman, the leaders, the boss,
standing up there when the wave hits the rock,
passing out faith and confidence like life jackets,
knowing the currents, holding the doubts,
imagining the delights and terrors of every landfall;
captain, pirate and parent by turns,

the bearer of our countless hopes and expectations.
We give them our trust. We give them our effort.
What we ask in return is that they stay true.

— William Ayot

How can this be? How can leadership be described in so few words? Is it really that simple? Yes, it is. But it's also true that a leader will spend his or her entire career trying to live up to this one simple request of *staying true*.

One client I worked with never ceased to amaze me with his ability to meet this deeper expectation. If you asked his people what this meant to them, they would undoubtedly agree with these kinds of descriptions:

• *He loves his work. If anything he gets down in the weeds a little too much. However, every one of his team members finds his pleasure in doing the actual work itself to be inspiring.*

• *Although he might not use the word 'love,' that's exactly how he felt about his people. One of the ways he demonstrated that love was often putting himself at financial and political risk to protect them.*

So can we actually describe what it means to stay true? I believe it's tied to the definition of great leadership from Chapter 1: *love shown twice*. It means we love the vision in which we're investing our professional lives. That is, the work being done and, more to the point, the benefit that work is providing to others.

Secondly, it's loving the people who are called to the vision along side the leader. It is trusting and supporting those people. It is giving ample room and freedom as described

in one of our great sources of wisdom, the *Tao Te Ching*:
It loves and nourishes all things, but does not lord it over them.

Staying true also means granting people the dignity of having motivations beyond a paycheck. Again, it's obvious that one of the critical reasons people work is to earn money to support themselves. But do we believe that people are so *one-dimensional* as to only, or even primarily, work for money?

Yes, of course some jobs may be so boring, onerous and/or poorly designed that people feel deadened and numb. In such cases, where money is the only reward, of course it rises to the top of people's minds and concerns.

Fortunately, there is some work out there that is both satisfying and rewarding. We must conclude that no one is simply coin operated. The poem puts it this way:

not because we are paid,
not because we can see some advantage,

The poem goes on. Business magazines are filled with the glowing pictures of leaders who are invariably pictured at the height of their glory and triumph, benefiting from all their hard work and smart decisions. No doubt these are admirable and necessary traits, however the poem talks about other leadership traits we admire that are beyond these necessary (but not sufficient) attributes.

not because of what they have accomplished,
not even because of the dreams they dream,
but simply because of who they are:
the man, the woman, the leaders, the boss,
standing up there when the wave hits the rock,

It's been said that we can walk a thousand miles within one single line of a good poem. Here are such lines that we can use and use again. Perhaps it is an overstatement to say faith and confidence can be *passed out* to others. It is true, however, that both faith and confidence have the qualities of a virus. Others can catch them if the virus is strong and persistent enough.

> *passing out faith and confidence like life jackets,*
> *knowing the currents, holding the doubts,*

No leader worth their salt speaks of a destination only in terms of its delights. Yes, of course they are real and, like a magnet, they pull us toward them. But there are terrors there, too.

> *imagining the delights and terrors of every landfall;*
> *captain, pirate and parent by turns,*
> *the bearer of our countless hopes and expectations.*

And then we are privy to the intimate trust that binds team members and their leaders.

> *We give them our trust. We give them our effort.*
> *What we ask in return is that they stay true.*

What's at Stake?

The bookshelves of the world groan under the weight of leadership books making uncountable claims about what it takes to be a good leader. Maybe it is as simple as "staying true" to one's self. Maybe that is all we need to do.

Questions for Your Journal

1. How and when can you use this poem as a *search and rescue* tool?

2. What questions does this poem raise for you?

3. Reflect on a person you look to as a shining example of *staying true* and why.

4. When you think of yourself as *staying true*, what does that mean?

5. What will you do differently after experiencing this poem, and what difference will it make?

A Betrayal in the Mind

"We are each other's harvest; we are each other's business; we are each other's magnitude and bond."

— Gwendolyn Brooks

I asked my client if there was a difference between agreeing with someone and understanding them. She looked at me funny and confirmed that she, of course, knew the difference. She gave me a quick description of each scenario, to which I quickly nodded yes.

Of course, we all know this, don't we? Still, my experience is that we conflate these two states regularly. We do that for a simple reason. It's because we are afraid that if we say we *understand* someone, that person will then jump to the conclusion that we also *agree* with him or her.

The tragedy is, this stops the process of understanding each other dead it its tracks. Truth is, people certainly don't like it when we *disagree* with them, but they are incensed if we refuse to *understand* them. Think about it for a moment. Have you ever made this or a similar statement to someone, *I just don't understand how you could think that way."* Often the real truth is we do *understand* their point, we just don't *agree* with it.

Until we are willing to really listen to the other person and see the world from their point of view, we are going to be susceptible to all sorts of problems, conflicts distortions and miscommunications.

One of the hardest things to do is hear someone describing a perspective or opinion that we do not agree with and remain calm, attentive and respectful. And, especially to refrain from jumping into the fray with our own opinion long before the other person is finished describing theirs. What can we do to remember what we already know, even when we're chomping at the bit to tell the other person our opinion?

Here is a poem that has proven itself in all manner of stress-filled situations. I've used it on many occasions with leaders and teams who needed to slow down just a tad to really listen and yes, understand and learn from each other.

A Ritual to Read to Each Other

If you don't know the kind of person I am
and I don't know the kind of person you are
a pattern that others made may prevail in the world
and following the wrong god home we may miss our star.

For there is many a small betrayal in the mind,
a shrug that lets the fragile sequence break
sending with shouts the horrible errors of childhood
storming out to play through the broken dyke.

And as elephants parade holding each elephant's tail,
but if one wanders the circus won't find the park,
I call it cruel and maybe the root of all cruelty
to know what occurs but not recognize the fact.

And so I appeal to a voice, to something shadowy,
a remote important region in all who talk:
though we could fool each other, we should consider —
lest the parade of our mutual life get lost in the dark.

For it is important that awake people be awake,
or a breaking line may discourage them back to sleep;
the signals we give—yes or no, or maybe —
should be clear: the darkness around us is deep.

— William Stafford

Leadership Is Long Term

The stakes could not be higher. Without building the kind of culture this poem implies, leaders, teams and whole organizations are vulnerable to the ravages of chronic misunderstandings and low-trust relationships that arise over time. In these environments, true understanding of each other is not solid enough for sustained good performance.

If you don't know the kind of person I am
and I don't know the kind of person you are
a pattern that others made may prevail in the world
and following the wrong god home we may miss our star.

As soon as we actually talk to one another, many of the problems fade. But if we are going to merely stand back and accept the assumptions that we and others have, then our chances of working together well shrink.

For there is many a small betrayal in the mind,
a shrug that lets the fragile sequence break
sending with shouts the horrible errors of childhood
storming out to play through the broken dyke.

Who could blame us for wanting things to work with expediency? Why go into difficult territory if we do not have to? Why question, when we can simply go along? But what if not asking one tough question results in a much tougher question coming right on its heels? What if we see something that does not match our values or the values of our organization and just shrug it off?

> *And as elephants parade holding each elephant's tail,*
> *but if one wanders the circus won't find the park,*
> *I call it cruel and maybe the root of all cruelty*
> *to know what occurs but not recognize the fact.*

At the heart of an ethical organization that values individuals understanding one another is a willingness to recognize what is happening as it is occurring and having the courage to speak out, describing what is seen.

> *And so I appeal to a voice, to something shadowy,*
> *a remote important region in all who talk:*
> *though we could fool each other, we should consider —*
> *lest the parade of our mutual life get lost in the dark.*

Of course there are clever methods of influence and other kinds of negotiation techniques, but that is not the point. The point is that we not fool each other, even if we can. The point is that we not get *lost in the dark.*

> *For it is important that awake people be awake,*
> *or a breaking line may discourage them back to sleep;*
> *the signals we give—yes or no, or maybe —*
> *should be clear: the darkness around us is deep.*

As we've already noted there is a huge difference between *understanding* someone and *agreeing* with that person. Perhaps the most skillful thing this poem reminds us to do, is to approach others in a skillful way that results in a true and deeper understanding. That is, to commit to fully listening to another person, doing our very best to *"know the kind of person"* they are. For example, we might say:

> *"Listen, our relationship is far more important than any one conversation or decision. It's therefore critical that I understand exactly how you feel and think about this issue. I'm not sure if we're going to agree on all or even any points regarding this matter, but I certainly want to ensure we understand fully your perspective and opinion before we take any substantive steps."*

What's at Stake?

The usefulness of this poem goes far beyond the surface success of our business enterprise, although of course that is critical. It speaks to the value of *deeper understanding* in all areas of our lives. It goes to some of the most profound challenges we face in our communities, nation and culture at large.

In the end, it is easier than we would like to believe to simply check out and stop listening to and understanding each other. Naturally, we are all busy and it takes time, energy and focus to more fully understand others. But in the end, no matter how busy we are it's imperative that we listen deeply to each other.

After all, without staying connected, communicating effectively and understanding each other more fully, *the darkness around us is indeed deep.*

Questions For Your Journal

1. Where do you go from here?

2. Are there places in which you might apply this poem in your current relationships? Do you need to go back and clean anything up?

3. What is your next step?

Why Gratefulness Matters Hugely
for Leaders

*In daily life we must see that it is not happiness
that makes us grateful, but gratefulness
that makes us happy.*

— David Steindl-Rast

There are two distinct kinds of gratefulness, even though we use a single word for both. Of the two, one is easy and one is hard. How we handle each type, especially the hard kind, will largely determine the level of happiness and success we experience both in our work and home lives.

Take a moment to consider all the things in your life for which you are absolutely, and without qualification, grateful. And if you really take the time to notice, and perhaps do a little journaling, you may find yourself experiencing more gratitude by the moment, as your list gets longer and longer.

For example, let's name just a few of the things for which we are immediately and spontaneously grateful—friends, loved ones, delicious food, and good work. Depending on how we're built, we might also include music, art, travel, books, and amazing sunsets in our list. For most of us, these are on the easy side of the gratefulness ledger.

But then there are the things in our lives that we would never choose. The hard and difficult things that happen to us, such as sickness, loss, failure, violence and all the ways our hearts can be broken. And also the normal day-to-day stumbles, mishaps and disappointments. So what do we do with these parts of our lives?

Perhaps surprisingly, one response is gratefulness—the second kind. And no, of course I don't mean that we are grateful for the difficult thing or disappointment itself. But rather we are grateful for the *opportunity* this challenging or even tragic event has created in our lives. The opportunity to grow, learn, heal, and become stronger and more resilient. And grateful for the courage to perhaps have our heart broken and still move on, still continue to love, still be thankful.

For me, poetry helps with both kinds of gratefulness. It helps me celebrate the easier kind of gratitude that is related to events that naturally bring joy and happiness. And with the second, more fierce and paradoxical gratitude, it helps me immeasurably as well.

In a real sense, poetry helps me integrate everything in my business and home life, from the most wonderful to the most difficult. For me, poetry has always been a special kind of practical support system for remembering my larger *self*, especially in the midst of a trial. Poetry provides tools for connecting *me to me*. And *me to others* and to the great big, magnificent, *mysterious other* all around us. Here's a poem I wrote that points toward some of these feelings.

Gratefulness

Each day the engine of my gratefulness
must be coaxed and primed into action.
Of course like any old clunker,

it would just as soon stay put.
For even after the labored start beats the inertia,
and the plume of white smoke struggles upward,
the same hills always appear,
soaring daily – tall and ominous as before.

There is the long slow hill of "aging"
so gradual and smooth at first.
And then that steep grade called "the news."
Yes, and always some mountain of a war
looming out there, never too far in the distance.

Even an old idea or a feeling long abandoned
might conspire to halt this fragile progress –
valves sputtering, tires flattening, clutch slipping.
But the old "potato, potato, potato" sound
of the engine, and all its mysterious fuel,
for which I am truly grateful
somehow
keeps stumbling along.

— Dale Biron

The first thing this piece reminds us, is that gratefulness is an ongoing practice, not some state that we blissfully arrive at and stay. In fact, the half-life of feeling grateful can often be quite short.

What's at Stake?

One of my long-time mentors, especially regarding the practice of gratefulness, is Brother David Steindl-Rast who is fond of saying, *"In daily life we must see that it is not happiness that makes us grateful, but gratefulness that makes us happy."*

But as leaders, why would we care about this business of happiness, or gratefulness for that matter? Well, first of all happy workers are more productive in general. And secondly, research has shown that leaders and team members who have a gratefulness practice and a general stance of gratitude are more creative, resilient, collaborative and a host of other goodies that make productivity soar and success more likely.

Questions for Your Journal

1. What are you grateful for in your life right now?

2. What example of paradoxical gratitude can you think of?

3. In what ways did you grow and learn from your paradoxical gratitude event?

A Beautiful Baffled Mind

*I had nothing to offer anybody
except my own confusion.*

— Jack Kerouac

One of the most powerful things any leader can say to his or her team is:

"I'm not sure what the answer is here—maybe you all can figure it out."

Sitting in on numerous team meetings over the years, I've observed only the most confident and capable leaders, saying such a thing. It's not, of course, that these leaders were not smart and capable. Rather, it was their willingness to:

- Be open and vulnerable with their team.

- Let others shine, grow and create their own solutions.

- Be comfortable with not always having the answer. It's the paradoxical ability to turn not knowing and even bafflement into a benefit to be embraced rather than a vulnerability to be avoided.

Yes, of course leaders get paid for having answers. But when they constantly have *all* the answers, that's another thing completely. Having *all* the answers means others are expected to simply standby while the leader does the problem solving and creative thinking for everyone else.

The Opposite of Having All The Answers Is Having Some of the Questions

Great leaders do not have all the answers. They know it's the quality of their questions and patience with allowing others resolve those questions that really separates average from good, or even great, leaders. And besides, regardless of other considerations, we know that preempting our team from coming up with solutions is the fastest way to hinder the team's growth, as well as their ability and desire to take on greater and greater responsibility.

But we can know something intellectually and never have that understanding reach our hearts, which is to say, it is unlikely we will ever change our behavior. This poem is one of my secret weapons when it comes to not just normalizing confusion, but also taking the strategic value of its sibling, *bafflement*, to a new level. It's a powerful search and rescue poem for the right situation.

The Real Work

It may be that when we no longer know what to do
we have come to our real work,
and that when we no longer know which way to go
we have come to our real journey.
The mind that is not baffled is not employed.
The impeded stream is the one that sings.

— Wendell Berry

Again, though we may know intellectually that we as leaders do not need all the answers, we often judge ourselves (quite harshly) when we don't have them. This poem says don't worry so much about not having the answer. In fact, is suggests there is real value in *not knowing*.

It Happens For Teams Too!

Of course, our discomfort with *not knowing* happens at the team level as well. When we first set out to resolve a problem as a team, we are often focused, on-track and strategic. Everyone on the team agrees that new answers to significant problems are needed. But then when those answers begin to come, often all the old roadblocks appear as well. Why? The long familiar stream of *but-that-won't-work* married to *yes-but* comments begin to flood in, along with the realization that there are nearly as many points-of-view in the room as there are people.

That's when frustration begins to grow. Some want to speed things up, while others want to slow down the process. The great temptation is to simply call it quits on the creative-thinking process. That's when we often retreat to our last idea, whether or not it provides any real improvement or solution. Of course confusion is no picnic.

But these moments of bafflement are critical for any leader and team to open to new or unexpected possibilities. Retreat to what is safe and known and nothing gets better. Continue on with the process and perhaps suffer the pain of wasted time, confusion, ruffled feathers and still make no prog-ress. There are no guarantees—however, retreating from confusion often means no real answers or progress. The question is, might there be a better way to move forward?

The Normalization of Frustration (& Bafflement)

While it's natural to be frustrated in this circumstance, maybe the poem is right. Perhaps if we can hang in there with a decent process just a little bit longer, we can run smack into a creative breakthrough. As we have said, there are no guarantees, but we know that turning that "*impeded stream*" into singing is what is demanded of leaders and teams now more than ever.

In fact, no one described these kinds of breakthroughs better than Oliver Wendell Holmes Jr. when he said, "*I would not give a fig for the simplicity this side of complexity, but I would give my life for the simplicity on the other side of complexity.*"

And having watched leaders and teams for many years, I have never seen anyone reach this level of discovering the new, creative and elegant solution without first grappling with complexity, simplicity and yes, even a required bit of confusion and bafflement.

What's at Stake?

Ultimately, this chapter is about humility, which is what it takes to first accept that *we do not know something* and are actually just a little baffled. This admission allows us to take on that *not knowing* stance as a strategic advantage. For leaders, it's a strategic advantage because we get to share the work of solving tough and interesting challenges with others who have so much to offer. Additionally, our team members may never get the chance to develop and contribute their talents, strengths and gifts unless we invite them to do so.

Questions For Your Journal

1. Where are you facing an *impeded stream* in your work or life right now?

2. Where might you apply this poem in your personal and work life?

3. What do you imagine your real work to be at this point in your life?

4. What about the real work of us all?

5. Is there an intersection where those two kinds of work merge?

6. When have you experienced doing good work, despite being constrained, confused and even baffled?

How to Make Frightening Requests
(of Ourselves)

"The fears we don't face become our limits."

— Robin Sharma

What is the request your life is making of you?

The first time I heard this question, I remember feeling a mix of curiosity, excitement and confrontation. I thought, what is my own answer to this question? Do I have such a request that I am willing to describe, claim or even admit? And if I have one, or more than one, might they be too small, average or tedious to be worth the effort required? In other words, *is the game worth the candle?*

In the absence of our own articulated request, certainly as business people and leaders, any number of readymade *requests* are provided. For example:

- How can we stay vital and profitable?
- How can we out perform the competition?
- How can we maximize profits and control our market?

These are valid concerns for any leader. But what happens as we move deeper into our careers and lives? What happens when our concernes grow more nuanced and complex? What happens when our bottom line is no longer one-dimensional, and begins to take on issues beyond profit and market dominance?

What happens when some of our core values (and the inherent requests they make of us) are called into question by the organizations we work with or for? For example, what happens when our current economic assumptions are proven to be suspect, even by the most cursory thought experiments? Perhaps, this is best summed up by the colorful British economist, Kenneth Boulding: *"Anyone who believes in indefinite growth in anything physical, on a physically finite planet, is either mad or an economist."*

Confronted by such realities as global warming and the increasing worldwide wealth gap, do we simply stay the course with our default cultural requests? I mean the kind that fall in line with, and support, our most common assumptions?

For example:

- More is better.

- Maximizing our own position is the only thing we need worry about.

- Pollution is simply the social cost of prosperity that individuals can ignore.

Of course, who could blame us for staying abstract and at 30-thousand feet with these matters? I mean who are we as individuals to make any real difference, in such huge and daunting matters?

But then comes along a poem like this one from David Whyte with its beautiful imagery, sensory cues and fierce statement.

SOMETIMES

Sometimes
if you move carefully
through the forest,

breathing
like the ones
in the old stories,

who could cross
a shimmering bed of leaves
without a sound,

you come
to a place
whose only task

is to trouble you
with tiny
but frightening requests,

conceived out of nowhere
but in this place
beginning to lead everywhere.

Requests to stop what
you are doing right now,
and

to stop what you
are becoming
while you do it,

questions
that can make
or unmake
a life,

questions
that have patiently
waited for you,

questions
that have no right
to go away.

— David Whyte

Whyte is famous for claiming something central and vital for the art of poetry in our work and personal lives. He refers to poetry as *"Language against which we have no defenses."*

So yes, what defenses do we have when we witness things that satisfy one critical value, yet go directly against other values we also hold dear? I have no easy or ready answers for this. I have acted far less than courageously in this world more times than I would like to admit. And yet, there have been certain occasions …

As is so often the case, my clients have shown the way, modeling with their actions and feet this bold willingness to accept their own frightening requests. Not pushing away critical requests, no matter how fierce.

I'm remembering the leader client who stood up for his team in the wake of organizational changes that he considered both short sighted and unfair. Who would have blamed him for going along with senior management who, after all were running fast and scared?

Why would he take such a risky stance that could have easily cost him his job? After all, even his own people felt that he had no choice. At least not until he demanded the choice by his courageous stand in the face of what he felt was wrong.

Even though this leader was not able to protect all of his people on every issue, his team had nothing but admiration and respect for him. Even the ones who were essentially forced out, knew that their leader had done everything he could, including taking on every request, frightening or otherwise that came his way.

What's at stake?

Boldness. If it is true that our *tiny but frightening requests*, will indeed never go away, then it is up to us to meet our challenges and their existence with as much boldness as possible. Goethe said, *"Whatever you can do or dream you can, begin it. Boldness has genius, power and magic in it."* If it is possible for us to spend a lifetime ignoring even those requests that will not go away, surely there is a profound cost in that ignorance. This David Whyte poem is a wonderful tool of remembrance, a true search and rescue tool for the heart and soul.

Questions For Your Journal

1. How can you best use this poem?
2. Are there requests that you have avoided?
3. What requests are they?
4. What now?

How To Be a Person First

*Serving requires us to know that our humanity is
more powerful than our expertise.*

— Rachel Naomi Remen, M.D

What does it mean to be a good leader? Is it the number
and quality of the ideas we have? Is it our IQ? Or perhaps
our EQ, emotional quotient? Does being creative and
clever make us a good leader? Perhaps it's our ability to
negotiate? And, of course, what about our successes and
wins? Do our triumphs make us good leaders?

No doubt, all these things impact the quality and effective-
ness of our leadership. When team members, clients and
colleagues take our measure, surely they consider some or
all of these qualities.

But let's travel even further back upstream to a more foun-
dational place. Where do these qualities actually come
from? In other words, how do we define the platform upon
which all the things we need to be and do as leaders occur?

In my experience this platform is far simpler to grasp than
we typically make it out to be. I just call it *being a person* ...

Let's take a moment to explore how poet William Staf-
ford defines this most fundamental aspect of anyone who
is an effective leader:

Being a Person

Be a person here. Stand by the river, invoke
the owls. Invoke winter, then spring.
Let any season that wants to come here make its own
call. After that sound goes away, wait.

A slow bubble rises through the earth
and begins to include sky, stars, all space,
even the outracing, expanding thought.
Come back and hear the little sound again.

Suddenly this dream that you are having matches
everyone's dream, and the result is the world.
If a different call came there wouldn't be any
world, or you, or the river, or the owls calling.

How you stand here is important. How you
listen for the next things to happen. How you breathe.

— William Stafford

In a way, it seems too simple that being a good or even great leader depends on something so basic. And yet, there is advice in this poem that is radically different from what most of us hear and experience every day.

I mean in a world obsessed with checking off one *to-do* item after another as fast as we can, we are told in the last line of the first stanza to simply … *wait*. Yes, we are told to wait. But wait for what?

Maybe it is that slow bubble rising through the earth that we must wait for.

A slow bubble rises through the earth
and begins to include sky, stars, all space,
even the outracing, expanding thought.
Come back and hear the little sound again.

I suggest we travel through these four lines of the second stanza as lightly as possible. Don't worry about analysis so much as letting the words and images simply do what they will. Then we can meet again in the third stanza.

Suddenly this dream that you are having matches
everyone's dream, and the result is the world.
If a different call came there wouldn't be any
world, or you, or the river, or the owls calling.

Of course this third stanza can send us down many different paths of meaning. But what is clear is that how we feel and think about the world is critical. And if what we think and feel about the world is synchronized with others, then our capacities and power as an individual and as a team are magnified many times over.

But then at the end of this poem comes the greatest payoff.

How you stand here is important. How you
listen for the next things to happen. How you breathe.

These are the things your people have always watched and noticed and calibrated about your leadership, even if they themselves did not know they were doing it. Are you present and in the moment? Do you look and listen for the inspiration emanating from within those you lead? These are the things that make you first a person and then a leader.

What's at Stake?

I will answer the question in this way … *everything*. I would say that being a person is a task that slowly comes over us if we let it. I would say that being a person has more to do with the *being* part of us and is less about the *doing* part. However if the *being* part is right, then the *doing* will almost always be productive and yes … good.

Of course, on one level we are all already people. However, poet William Stafford reminds us here that there are deeper, more courageous levels of person-hood. He reminds us that even the smallest things can make all the difference. He reminds us that standing, listening and breathing are all critical. In this way, being a person is something much more that just being in a human body. Rather, it is standing up, going deeper, and taking more responsibility for what it means to be human.

Questions For Your Journal

1.What does being a person mean to you?

2.How often do you give yourself that chance to simply wait, stand and breathe?

3.If it is true, as Shakespeare said, that we are all making up and living a dream that we call life … What is your dream?

When to Let Your Heart Decide

*Let yourself be silently drawn by the strange pull of
what you really love. It will not lead you astray.*

— Jalaluddin Rumi

Several years ago, the poem featured in this chapter scurried onto a page of my notebook during one of my morning writing sessions. Later I realized it must have bubbled up from a recent conversation with a psychotherapist friend about how challenging it can be to keep our deepest promises. I mean the ones we make to ourselves.

In our conversation, we ranged over many such vows. Like ones we make for exercising more or eating a healthier diet. Or perhaps that promise we make to work smarter and more creatively. And especially those really hard promises regarding our closest relationships at work and home. You know, that self-pledge not to be so hardheaded about being right, that sort of thing.

Soon our talk roamed into the specific challenge of preventing our mood and physiology and especially our inner critic from ganging up on us at the same time. Because they often muscle in and wrest away essential decisions about the running of our lives. *(Think perfect storm: Bad mood meets fight-or-flight response meets inner critic!)*

Not wanting to leave ourselves in such despair, my friend and I felt a surge of ambition and turned our thoughts toward more hopeful things. That is, we talked about a kind of cure. How we must recognize, then get down below the sometimes-hurtful vagaries of our current mood.

Next, we talked about burrowing down even deeper into the physiology of our bodies, where stress hormones like adrenalin and cortisol can conspire to be in charge.

And finally, we concluded we must sink down even deeper, where the voice of our *inner critic* lurks—the singularly unhelpful voice that keeps us in one rut or another.

In fact, it's just beyond this deepest place inside each of us where I believe our courage lies. The *"cor"* in courage is the ancient word for heart. So it is courage that both points toward and then allows us to follow the innermost feelings of our heart, as in our overarching *search and rescue mission for the heart* metaphor.

This can make the vital difference in our not winding up in some alienated cul-de-sac of shame or fear or guilt that keeps us depressed and stuck. Versus the courageous decision (and move) to wonderfully overwhelm our lives with the connected joy, surprise, and healing potential of each moment.

Because when this happens and the heart rules, we are far more likely to lead our team skillfully, take that walk, write that story or poem, make that change at work, resist *being right*, paint, meditate, and yes even forgo that sugary treat.

Of course, knowing my own weakness for words and my advanced case of *Adult-Onset Poetry Syndrome*, I couldn't help but think about having a few poems around to help this heart-directed process. And yes, as a coach I keep these around constantly.

After all, it was writer Anne Lamott who coined one of my favorite guiding mantras: *"My mind is a bad neighborhood I try not to go into alone."*

Here is a poem I'm including in my own neighborhood-taming, first-aid kit for handling the normal emergencies of life. Because at times we all get bullied, battered or simply confused. That's when we most need to remember … *let heart decide.*

Decisions

Mood says, whatever it wants.
Body says, I'm too tired.
Inner critic says, only no.
Heart says, let me decide.
Courage looks down at the
ground, tracing a toe in the dust,
then stutters, and quietly confides:
Yes, let heart decide …

— Dale Biron

What's at Stake?

Naturally we all want to be more resilient. And letting our hearts decide is really what it all comes down to. Our linear, logical mind, after all is what we need to implement the most complex and critical strategies in our work and home lives. However, no matter how gifted, necessary and great the mind is at *making* things happen, it is the heart's domain to decide on *what should* happen.

What are your own unique signals that it is time consult your heart for an important decision? Of course, our ego-self can be loud, persuasive and pervasive. This brief poem for your leadership toolkit is intended to allow your heart to talk back to your mood, body, critic and mind. This is a poem-tool that actually recognizes the strengths of our minds, but also the strengths of our hearts.

Remember, let heart decide …

Questions for Your Journal

1. What do you do to help your mood when it needs helping?

2. What part of you most often makes your decisions?

3. When have you been the most courageous?

4. What decision have you recently made that you want to revisit now?

5. Who in your life is your mentor for making heart-based decisions?

6. The great scientist of our interior selves, Sigmund Freud once said: *"Everywhere I go, I find a poet has been there before me."* What do you suppose Freud meant by that, and what does it mean when it comes to letting your heart decide?

Why Only Kindness Makes Sense

*Kindness is more important than wisdom, and the
recognition of this is the beginning of wisdom.*

— Theodore Isaac Rubin

Few things depress and confuse us like *random acts of violence*. Of course, when someone commits violence while stealing money or possessions, we have a ready-made bucket of understanding to place it in. At least we can say, *"It's not senseless violence,"* where the only explanation we can imagine is that someone is either insane or driven by a wicked brew of hurt, bitterness, prejudice and hate.

These *random acts of violence* exist at the opposite end of the spectrum from love and kindness, and as far away as one can get.

So, we invented the term *random acts of kindness*, which breaks through our awareness to surprise and delight us. Why? Because as humans, we imagine that such acts of kindness, untethered to reciprocity, are motivated by some wonderful combination of joy, gratitude, generosity and love.

Of course, we know that kindness rarely makes it into the formal strategic plans of teams and organizations. It's not that we don't want or appreciate kindness; it's more that we don't think it can be looked at strategically or with much intention. I beg to differ.

Over the years, I've given the following poem to many leaders. I've used it at planning meetings, team-building presentations, and often in one-on-one coaching sessions.

With very little preamble, I often just present the poem.

Are you ready?

Kindness

Before you know what kindness really is
you must lose things,
feel the future dissolve in a moment
like salt in a weakened broth.
What you held in your hand,
what you counted and carefully saved,
all this must go so you know
how desolate the landscape can be
between the regions of kindness.
How you ride and ride
thinking the bus will never stop,
the passengers eating maize and chicken
will stare out the window forever.

Before you learn the tender gravity of kindness,
you must travel where the Indian in a white poncho
lies dead by the side of the road.
You must see how this could be you,
how he too was someone
who journeyed through the night with plans
and the simple breath that kept him alive.

Before you know kindness as the deepest thing inside,
you must know sorrow as the other deepest thing.
You must wake up with sorrow.

You must speak to it till your voice
catches the thread of all sorrows
and you see the size of the cloth.

Then it is only kindness that makes sense anymore,
only kindness that ties your shoes
and sends you out into the day to mail letters and purchase bread,
only kindness that raises its head
from the crowd of the world to say
it is I you have been looking for,
and then goes with you every where
like a shadow or a friend.

— Naomi Shihab Nye

Most leaders like this poem. They're fascinated by its message—however, few have thought of kindness the way it's described. Even fewer have considered taking the attitudinal stance and course of action to do what the poem suggests. That is, to build our own kindness muscles, we must notice all the places where kindness does not exist, or exists in meager quantities.

Truth is, kindness, like food and water, is essential. It is not fragile at all. Kindness has sharp elbows and can take care of itself if we let it. And by saying that, I mean it can fend for itself, if we do as the amazing poet Naomi Shihab Nye suggests. We can transform ourselves if we will simply recognize that: *Before you know kindness as the deepest thing inside, / you must know sorrow as the other deepest thing.*

Soon, you will be taken to a whole list of new and exciting questions: What does kindness mean to you as a person and as a leader? When was the last time you acted with kindness? What are the conditions that most often lead you to be kind to others? How often do you respond in a kind way in your personal life? What about your work life? Do you notice others responding back to you in similarly kind ways?

What's at Stake?

As leaders within our organizations, we know the old tired approaches are falling away. We no longer need to relegate such kindness only to our non-work interactions. They matter in all areas of our lives. Kindness matters to us as leaders because we are entering an incredibly tumultuous and challenging time in our work lives. We are entering a time when careers and jobs are being destroyed much faster than they are being created. We are entering a time when the essential goodwill that we hold for each other will play a huge role in our organizational futures and fortunes. Which is to say, we must be terribly *kind* to one another, if we are to meet the daunting challenges we are facing.

Questions for Your Journal

1. How can you put this poem to work for you and your team?

2. When it comes to growing and supporting *kindness*, what should you do first?

3. What should you do second, then next and next and next and next

Leading Between the Rocks and Hard Places

Choices are always Hobson's choices. All you have to do is get a little more alert to see that even your best moves are compromises—and complicated.

— William Stafford

Our natural impulse is to force ourselves toward making the perfect decision. We want to believe there is a single right answer for every challenge if we can simply bear down hard enough on all the various decision-making levers at our disposal. In fact, if we're having problems making a decision, we tend to think we simply need to get more logical, linear and analytical ... Right? Well, as it turns out, that's not always the case.

Here are three challenges derived from my work over the years that represent a *tip of the iceberg* look at the kind of *Hobsonian* choices leaders face each and every day.

The Challenge of the Oldest

A family business has three siblings who are set to take over the business during the next few years. Starting from the bottom of the ladder, they have all worked hard in the enterprise for years, each *earning their stripes* as the saying goes. They also have learned to be highly competitive with one another.

For various reasons of age and custom, the oldest sibling has a clear sense of having earned the right to eventually head up the company. For genuine reasons, this may not be best for the firm.

If the company founders, meaning the parents, do nothing, it seems clear that the path of least resistance will lead to the eldest child eventually taking charge. If they step in and overtly chart a different course, then it could cause even more problems with the relationships among the three siblings going forward.

A Job No One Wants

A leader plainly notices that a team member is struggling. Thoughtful, sincere steps are taken to help the person get back on the right track and succeed. But nothing seems to help the situation as the team member continues to struggle, complain, gossip and generally cause problems with others, as well as underperforming on their own core duties.

On one level, it seems simple, right? It is clearly time to let this person go. Of course that is one possibility. However, there are multiple layers in play. Here is more context.

This is an entry-level position with little to no glamour. In fact, it's essentially a maintenance job that involves a non-stop, hot, dusty and often smelly environment. And yes, it's also an essential, even critical role that has little or no room for being improved by re-structuring the work.

All this has made hiring for this position extremely difficult. Of course you can increase the pay. But because of how this job tightly fits in with others, there are constraints on how much money can be used to sweeten the pot. Plus, much research confirms that money, being an *extrinsic reward*, has serious limitations when it comes to long-term, sustained motivation.

The Cost of Grief on the Team

Meanwhile, in a different company and situation, a team member is also struggling. But in this case, there has been a tragic event in their life—a loved one close to them has died.

This person is excellent at his job. He also cares deeply, with a passion for his work that is palpable. However, the emotional toll of the extended grief presents a greater and greater challenge to him, and by extension to the rest of the team.

Who can say how much grief is the right amount for any one of us to experience? And who cannot understand how such pain might easily cause us to become *impatient with, snap at* and *quick to criticize co-workers?*

On the other hand, who could blame a team for wanting to function at a higher level, with everyone feeling safe from criticism, blame and peril? How exactly are we supposed to decide when neither option feels right?

When There Is No Good Answer

All three scenarios are similar in that they offer no clear answers or easy way forward. They seem only to offer a *"damned if you do, damned if you don't"* set of choices. Here's a poem that lives squarely in this difficult territory.

Traveling Through the Dark

Traveling through the dark I found a deer
dead on the edge of the Wilson River road.

It is usually best to roll them into the canyon:
that road is narrow; to swerve might make more dead.

By glow of the tail-light I stumbled back of the car
and stood by the heap, a doe, a recent killing;
she had stiffened already, almost cold.
I dragged her off; she was large in the belly.

My fingers touching her side brought me the reason—
her side was warm; her fawn lay there waiting,
alive, still, never to be born.
Beside that mountain road I hesitated.

The car aimed ahead its lowered parking lights;
under the hood purred the steady engine.
I stood in the glare of the warm exhaust turning red;
around our group I could hear the wilderness listen.

I thought hard for us all—my only swerving —,
then pushed her over the edge into the river.

— William Stafford

What's at Stake?

Traveling Through the Dark provides another powerful search and rescue tool for the heart and soul. Like any good poem, it allows us to walk inside and have our own experience. In this case, it's the experience of being cast headlong into a seemingly no-win dilemma. And if as leaders, the linear and logical parts of ourselves pretend they're all that's needed for such decisions, then the strong emotions evoked by this poem can help remind us of a larger, more nuanced world.

As leaders we are constantly asked to work with dilemmas like those described above. We need tools to help us sort them out. And one of those tools, quite frankly, is simply to *retreat and rejuvenate* on a regular basis. Of course, there is no magic any leader can do to avoid these kinds of situations. There are certainly structured ways, however, to take the time to think, grow and ultimately feel our way into the right decision.

Another wise tool is to go as far *back upstream* as possible. That is, to go to the source of the challenge itself. This does not mean there is some easy trick to make the conundrums and dilemmas simply go away. It does mean that when we return to the source of the challenge itself, we can often see a wiser and more skillful way forward.

Questions for Your Journal

1. In each of the scenarios described above, what would it mean to *go back upstream* closer to the source of the challenge?

2. When faced with such a Hobson's choice in the past, how did you handle it?

3. What were the results of that decision?

4. What would you do differently today, if anything?

The Perfect Way to Procrastinate

"It's amazing how long it takes to complete something you're not working on."

— Unknown

Some leaders are haphazard. Their motto is: *fire, fire, fire!* They do not procrastinate but rather have the opposite challenge. They condense, cut out, abbreviate, and cut to the chase, often before they or anyone else even knows what is being chased.

Of course, operating this way is a problem, but many of us err more often on the other side. We wait. And we wait and wait, especially when deciding feels risky. Oh my God! What if we get it wrong? Our motto is: *ready, ready, ready!*

So what's underneath this procrastination dynamic? No doubt many things. But at the very core of the challenge, I believe every leader, like every artist, must come to terms with what I call the *vision gap*. This is the gulf between what we imagine in our *mind's eye* and what we can actually achieve in the world.

Do we get better over time at creating our visions with more fidelity? Yes. Does it help to learn (in this case) the craft and skills of leadership? Of course. Does practicing help? Yes, it helps without a doubt.

But there is still the sometimes-excruciating reality of the vision gap all leaders face. For example, when a leader gets a creative idea, there is an immediate image of what is possible. It's a vision of the reality that could be true. This, by the way, is an amazing and positive leadership skill. The ability to *envision new things* is a foundational characteristic of leadership, as it is in all forms of art.

The irony is that the better we are at envisioning new things and situations, the scarier it can feel to get started. That's because there is virtually no chance we're going to be able to create the reality exactly as we envision it ... *at least not at first.*

Now, to prime the pump on your own search and rescue mission, here is a poem that confronts the reality and contours of our own unique vision gaps.

Ode to Procrastination

*It is the long windup, the writer's perfectly
sharpened pencil, the artist's sun-drenched
room, that system for trying to control everything.
A getting ready to get ready, the air still, ripe and*

*perfect. An adoring crowd hushed in anticipation
and excitement, all things primed for action. You,
revived, rested, your opus achievement in sight.
But then the perfect puts a paw on the quivering*

*strings of your motivation: Suddenly, everything
you wanted leans in watching. It's quiet, spotlessly
planned, but now you long for the chaos of surprise.
You say, "Ah, hell with it" and just get started.*

— Dale Biron

Underneath this brief piece is a core layer of fear. I had to write the poem and present it to others to understand the underlying message. This often happens with art we create. Truth is that fear of *getting it wrong* is powerful. It can dig a well of perfection so deep that no coin thrown in will ever reach bottom.

We want our vision to be perfectly reflected in the products of our imaginations and labors. So we set about to have everything *just right* before we get around to beginning our work. But then as described in the poem, something shifts and another part of us wonderfully breaks through.

I believe the part of us that breaks through is this slightly cranky, rascally part of us that starts to feel cramped by all the *just rightness* we've created around us. Call it your inner Huckleberry Finn that bridles against too much pomp and preparation. It is that wild, untamed, untrammelled part of us that insists on having a say. It is that part of us that's more afraid of missing out than messing up. It is that part of us that just wants to get on with it!

What's at Stake?

Recklessly moving too fast, as we've already said, causes big problems at one end of the spectrum. However, at the opposite, perhaps more prevalent end, procrastination causes many other kinds of troubling challenges. There are the basic performance issues of missing deadlines. And yes, there are worthy projects and dreams that simply never happen or at least do not happen fully. These can lead to huge hits to our self-esteem and, ultimately, to our confidence and even our happiness.

Ultimately the goal is right in the middle, staying away from either extreme. This means we can procrastinate just enough to allow time for our creative skills and capacities to kick in. And it means we boldly move forward fast enough to get ourselves into action before the opportunity and harvest are both gone.

At times I fantasize the real answer may be the simple rhythm of doing what is *fun, hard, fun, hard, fun* … and so on. I do know that completion builds energy and that completing both fun and hard tasks is both necessary and invigorating.

What's at stake for all of us is *daring to begin*, no matter how difficult that process. And to continue creating no matter how fractured and flawed the manifestation of our vision can be at times. Because we must also never forget how wonderful and amazing the process of creating can be, especially for leaders.

Questions For Your Journal

1. Leonard Bernstein once said, *"To achieve great things, two things are needed: a plan and not quite enough time."* Where in your work and personal life is that combination perfectly balanced for you?

2. What are the circumstances in your life that conspire to have you procrastinate?

3. Could you purposely plan for imperfections in your project to give yourself the courage and *cover* to simply get started?

4. When it comes to procrastination, what other poems, stories or aphorisms do you need in your search and rescue kit?

THE TROUBLE WITH HERO-LEADERS

Unhappy the land that is in need of heroes.
— Bertolt Brecht

Without realizing it, most of us have internalized something I call the *hero-leader* myth. This happens not because we are egotistical—just the opposite. As good leaders, we want to be supportive and helpful. Unfortunately, while playing the role of the *hero-leader*, we are unlikely to actually be helpful and supportive.

In fact, *hero-leaders*, without realizing it, often do as much damage as good. Why? Because believing this myth has us believe that leaders ought to:

- Have all or most of the answers.
- Rarely be in doubt.
- Show little or no vulnerability.
- Have the ability to fix all problems, situations and even people.

Of course, for team members it's easy to see the other side of the coin. The mirror image of this myth in the mind of team members is to believe such things as:

- Heroes are braver, tougher and smarter than average folks like me.

- Heroes always have all the answers so I'll just wait to be told what to do.

- Without someone to save our team and company, we won't survive.

- Heroes are born brave, which is why they can do what they do.

Too often, the hero-leader myth sets everyone up for failure. Leaders are stressed out and besieged by trying to constantly pull off epic acts and feats of near magic. This can make us feel isolated and unappreciated. On the other hand, team members are cast into a passive role, simply waiting for *the answers* to be generated from above. Bottom line? No one is very happy or effective.

Do I mean all leaders? No, of course not. Leaders and team members are along a spectrum regarding these matters. The best leaders have pushed through this misunderstanding to a place of supporting their teams in much more wise and skillful ways. Similarly, many team members have bridled against this old paradigm and are not simply participating as passive *pairs of hands* just waiting to be told what to do. But it is also true that this *hero-leader* myth is very much alive and well and causing pain and missed opportunities for many leaders and team members.

Which brings me to a poem by William Stafford that can help any leader who is beginning to fall for the old hero-leader myth:

"It's heavy to drag, this big sack …"

It's heavy to drag, this big sack of what
you should have done. And finally
you can't lift it any more.

Someone says, "Come on," and you
just look at them. Trees are waiting,
mountains. You never intended
that it should come to this.

But Now has arrived and is looking
straight at you, the way a lion does
when thinking it over, and anything
can happen. It's time for the cavalry
or maybe the Lone Ranger. But they
won't come. Maybe the music will
spill over and start it all again.
Maybe.

— William Stafford

This poem takes a gentle and humorous poke at our idea of heroes. But the poke is also definite and intentional as well. It reminds us of both the hazards of being a hero, as well as the dangers of waiting for a hero to show up. As the old saying goes: *"We are the ones we've been waiting for."*

A New Kind of Hero

I would argue the real definition of a hero is someone who helps amplify the best and strongest capacities and strengths of another person. This kind of hero-leader frequently sees a bigger version of *others* ... than they see in themselves. That is the kind of *hero-leader* we all must strive to become!

Our featured poet for this chapter talks about an event that happened early in his life that can be very helpful for understanding the kind of hero we're talking about.

"I remember when I was a little kid, my father took me out for a hike in the country and we were looking for a

> *hawk that we thought had landed in a line of cottonwood*
> *trees … and he said, "Now Billy, look carefully in these*
> *trees. You may be able to see the hawk better than I can."*
> *For me, this is just a little emblem in my life … because*
> *I remember the jolt I felt: could I see the hawk before my*
> *father would? And his tone of voice just said, "Maybe you*
> *can, maybe you can't … give it a try."*

Robert Bly, philosopher, poet and extraordinary thinker-at-large once described this incident between William Stafford and his father as precisely the way you turn your child into an accomplished poet. And to that I would say this is also the way to build a curious and confident leader and person. After all, the opposite of a *hero-leader* is a *learner-leader* who is always ready to replace old strategies that are not working with new ones that are.

Imagine the feeling of confidence we could support and reinforce in others by such practices on our part. What if we said to a team member, *"Maybe your ideas for the project are best. See what you can come up with."* Then imagine what that kind of confidence might do for others in their development and achievements.

I would be hard-pressed to demonstrate a better example of a courageous *learner-leader* than with this brief story told by William Stafford about his dad. It, of course, takes great courage and self-confidence as a leader to first admit that we do not have all the answers and that others may actually surpass us in their skill or creativity. And yet when we are able to do this, we are doing exactly what it takes to help support the growth of that same confidence in others.

What's at Stake?

One of the most successful leaders I coached had a wonderful way of listening to others quietly as they described their dreams. For example, one team member wanted to study Tai Chi. This leader supported her in bringing the martial art to the company in a way that also proved deeply helpful to many other employees. I've seen this kind of simple, supportive empowerment time and time again, which effectively served the individuals and their teams, as well as the whole organization.

Questions for Your Journal

1. What are the essential assumptions you make regarding leader as hero?

2. How easy or difficult is it for you to do what William Stafford's dad did regarding who would see the hawk first?

3. As a leader how much pressure do you put on yourself to always have the right answer, create miracles and constantly pull the rabbit out of the hat?

4. Have you ever had a metaphorical lion stare you down?

5. If yes, what happened next?

How To Be an Emotionally Intelligent Leader

If your emotional abilities aren't in hand, if you
don't have self-awareness, if you are not able to
manage your distressing emotions, if you can't have
empathy and have effective relationships,
then no matter how smart you are,
you are not going to get very far.

—— Daniel Goleman

Do you know that old cliché about certain leaders? We say they are *loose cannons*, meaning they are volatile, with hair trigger emotions—emotions, such as anger in particular, that they have precious little awareness of, or control over.

Have you ever experienced a leader who was like that? The kind that *does not have ulcers … but is a carrier.* When we hear quips like this we have to laugh at least a little, even though the challenges they present are anything but funny.

In my experience, this type of leader represents the extreme end of the spectrum. But the truth is we all have the capacity to lose our way at times. We can become overwhelmed by a massive to-do list that we never seem able to complete. And with so many pushes and tugs on our attention and focus, we can lose our capacity for both awareness and, yes, even caring—at least at the level we need to care.

There's certainly no magic elixir for building the emotional intelligence that will work in every situation. However, it's also true that nothing can open our hearts like a good poem with powerful language that takes us to places where we are naturally more open and vulnerable.

I believe our emotions are like any other muscle that regularly needs a good workout. I'm not talking about anything fancy or exotic or that even takes very long. Here is a poem I've used with many leaders that speaks to something universal in many of our individual life experiences:

May

I wanted to stay with my dog
when they did her in
I told the young veterinarian
who wasn't surprised.
Shivering on the chrome table,
she did not raise her eyes to me when I came in.
Something was resolved in her.
Some darkness exchanged for the pain.
There were a few more words
about the size of her tumor and her age,
and how we wanted to stop her suffering,
or our own, or stop all suffering
from happening before us
and then the nurse shaved May's skinny leg
with those black clippers;
she passed the needle to the doctor
and for once I knew what to do
and held her head against mine.
I cleaved to that smell
and lied into her ear

that it would be all right.
The veterinarian, whom I'd fought
about when to do this thing
said through tears
that it would take only a few minutes
as if that were not a long time
but there was no cry or growl,
only the weight of her in my arms,
and then on the world.

— Bruce Weigl

A silent pause for reflection and a few deep breaths are called for after experiencing a poem such as this. So many of us have had or known beloved pets that it is easy to relate. This poem for me is wonderfully simple and profound at the same time.

With this subject, it could easily have slipped into a sentimentality that paradoxically wouldn't open our hearts and minds nearly as effectively. But the language is so grounded in the physical and so directly speaks to our senses that, in addition to the obvious sadness, it also calls up other more gentle emotions, such as tenderness and caring. Because having a pet is such a common experience, and because of the way those critters touch our hearts, this poem is a natural tool to remind us to stop and reconnect with our emotions and our humanity.

What's at Stake?

Wait, are we saying we should keep this poem strategically handy for those times when we are overwhelmed? Yes, but I mean a particular type of overwhelmed feeling. I mean that kind of overwhelm that descends on us when our heart is feeling heavy and disconnected. I mean that kind of overwhelm when we feel alienated from both our selves and others.

Perhaps even more than some of the other pieces in this book, this poem is a search and rescue mission for even deeper emotions of the heart. It is a call to the parts of us that extend compassion and empathy to others.

It is for any heart that has been unintentionally hardened by too much to do, too much to think about, and too much preventing us from staying focused on the single most critical thing for any leader... the core people and relationships we depend upon daily. This is why we must become emotionally intelligent leaders even when we are stressed and hassled. This is when we need tools to help us stop, reflect on the broader context of our lives, and yes, open up our hearts.

Questions for Your Journal

1. Did this poem open up your heart? In what ways?

2. What conspires to have you become less empathetic with others?

3. Considering the only way to change someone's mind is to connect with their heart, how will you do that?

4. What is the state of your core relationships in your home and work life?

5. How do you handle strong emotions when you have no time to process them?

ARE WE REALLY ON OUR OWN SIDE?

Like a lot of people, I've got a self-loathing streak
that's alive and well. It acts as a de facto engine
when I'm working, but it also has its
extraordinary pitfalls, too.

— Ryan Reynolds

If I could step through the pages of this book and become your living, breathing coach, one of the questions I would ask you is, *"In our work together, could you please pretend you're on your own side?"* Your first response would likely be laughter. Naturally we assume we're already on our own side. But is it true? Do we allow ourselves to be happy, have fun and celebrate our wins? Do we give ourselves the benefit of the doubt? The first lines from the poem *The Holy Longing* by Johann Wolfgang von Goethe may shed a little light on this territory (Dale Biron translation).

Tell only the wise or else be silent
For those who do not see will mock it straight away

Of course, the obvious request Goethe is making is for us to surround ourselves with wise people who understand us and will support our plans, especially our more adventurous ones. However, there is a second truth buried even deeper in these lines. It's that often our worst "mocking" critic is actually ourself. You know the old saying, "we are our own worst enemy." Here I believe Goethe is also suggesting that we tell our best ideas and plans *only* to the wisest parts of ourselves as well!

Writer Anne Lamott once said, "My mind is a bad neighborhood I try not to go into alone." This, too, almost always invokes a laugh or at least a chuckle. We laugh because we know the feeling of those repetitive dark places our minds can go to. Here's a poem I've used with many leaders that backs into a strange but genuine question. The poem reminds us that we can hit our personal *reset button* to forget what needs forgetting, so we can clear the decks to be happy and, quite simply, to operate as if we were *on our own side.*

Sun Trail

Look. The poppies
they are at it again
exploding on the
hills with their deep
yellow flames and
supple hearts.
The tender green pines
the red manzanita
the wild iris, low and steady –
they all breathe the
secrets of the dark soil
from where the poppies came.
And they bend slightly to praise
the golden parachutes
who in turn pour themselves
joyfully, opening
without restraint up and
toward the sun.

As the black bellied poppies
teach with tender care
how to close up shop
daily, to forget what
needs forgetting.
How not to shrink
from these sanguine
spring hills
at the first sign of
happiness.

— Dale Biron

What's at Stake?

Slowly and subtlety over time we can unwittingly train ourselves to be drawn to, and even addicted to feeling unhappy and out of sorts, even when there is no apparent reason. Or maybe the old reason has lingered so long it's turned us toward being a permanent victim of life. One symptom of this is an outsized amount of complaining and associated need for perfection. If we could only make things perfect enough in our lives, somehow we feel that would reverse all the previous hurts and losses.

But letting that fantasy go, there's good and hopeful news. Happiness itself is wonderfully subversive. In fact, nurturing the ability to handle more of it can become the opening we need to escape our self-imposed limitations.

This chapter's poem serves as a wakeup call for new awareness concerning what actually makes us happy. So then we can get about the business of doing things differently. As we say, awareness is critical and needed, but of course it's actually *behavior* that makes the sustained contribution.

This poem can act as a fast, simple search and rescue tool for your heart, especially when you forget that you have every right to be happy and that you can choose to be happy *(and be on your own side)* any time you wish to do so.

Questions For Your Journal

1. What is it about your work that makes you most happy?

2. How do you celebrate when what makes you happy … happens?

3. How do you recover when life seems to gang up on you?

How Much Is Enough?

We learn from our gardens to deal with the most
urgent question of our times.

— Wendell Berry

Every action we take in life and in business springs from an impulse of thought, the subtle recognition of an unfulfilled need, a quiet inner nudge—in other words, the seed of an idea. Once we become aware of it, we move forward with as much energy, creativity and resources as we can spare. How do we know when to back off, or even stop?

What's true is that actual seeds know exactly how much water, air, light and nutrients from the soil are needed—*and not an ounce more*—to grow the most amazing, delicious vegetables you've ever tasted. I'm talking about tomatoes, zucchini, cucumbers, arugula, lettuce, basil, kale and chard just to name the crowd of green groceries that populate my garden this year alone.

So what can we learn from our gardens as Wendell Berry suggests in the quote above? What can these timeless teachers tell us about the question of *how much is enough?* Of course, there are the mega versions of these questions concerning issues like global economies, wealth distribution and climate. But let's not stray from where everything must start, and that is with each of us personally: right here, right now, right in our own lives, backyards and businesses. My point is, if we can't answer this question personally, how will we ever be able to answer it at a cultural, societal and even global level?

So, as leaders, what do we watch out for when it comes to the balance of *not too much* and *not too little?* How much profit is enough? How many clients and how much growth is enough? How much personal time do we want to invest in our work lives as it relates to our family and loved ones, for example? What is the right amount of travel and time spent away from home?

How much meaning, purpose and satisfaction are enough? And of course once we start asking these kinds of questions, we can't help but venture to the other side of the coin by asking how much is too little as well?

Right in the sweet spot of our "how much is enough" question is a classic teaching story made famous in the 1960s by a German writer, Heinrich Böll. There have been many adaptations and versions of this tale, however it boils down to this:

> A successful businessperson tourist is visiting an idyllic little village on the sea. Gazing about, he spots a local inhabitant lying in a small fishing boat happily snoozing away in the sunshine. The tourist snaps a picture and the local fisherman wakes up. The tourist immediately strikes up a conversation. He observes to the fisherman that the weather is perfect for fishing and asks him, "Why aren't you out in your boat catching more fish?" Casually the fisherman answers, "Well, I had a great morning fishing and caught all I need."

To which the intrepid and enterprising tourist begins to describe a whole scenario of actions and events to the fisherman that conclude in the fisherman being rich and famous beyond his dreams. He would start by working harder every day, selling his extra fish and soon buying a larger boat. In no time the fisherman would have a whole fleet of boats, followed quickly by opening his own seafood plant, and then the sky would be the limit.

"And then, and then" asks the fisherman, "what would happen then?" "Well, of course having all that wealth and success and all those resources, your time would be your own," the excited tourist, responded. "You would be able to kick-back by the sea, doze when you wanted, appreciate the beautiful sea, and have no worries at all."

After a few awkward and revelatory moments of the fisherman looking confused, he said, "Oh, you mean like my life is now …"

I can think of few clients or friends who are in danger of going to a small fishing village to live. However, the point and questions raised by this story are real. Here is an odd little poem that came to me some years ago. I've used it with leaders and others to approach this mind-numbing question of how much is enough?

The Moral Dilemma of Yellow

Who decided on the color of traffic signals?
I'll admit that red is an exciting color,
and it does do strange things to our
nervous system. Perhaps it was always
destined to be the color of – don't go.

But what of green?
Why not blue or hot pink or turquoise even?
All these colors, it seems to me,
are perfectly capable of signaling the brain
to press down upon the gas pedal. But then
comes the most troubling question of all.
Why should yellow have been given the
entire burden of yield? Of slowly doing
less on purpose. Of not taking it all.
Of exercising even a modest restraint,
of asking that most irreverent and holy
question of all — how much is enough?

— Dale Biron

In Praise of Enoughers

We actually have a famous and revered mentor to call on here. It is our own George Washington. Writer and historian Garry Wills rightly observed that Washington achieved his greatness not as much for what *he did*, but from what *he did not do*.

King George III of the United Kingdom famously said that if George Washington retired from public life and returned to the farm at the height of his personal and political power, "he will be the greatest man in the world."

And that is exactly what Washington did. He did not consolidate, claim or maximize power. He did not do what every other glorious, celebrated and triumphant leader had done before him. He stepped back. He resigned, and then he retired to his farm.

An observation from Washington biographer James Thomas Flexner tells more: "In all history few men who possessed unassailable power have used that power so gently and self-effacingly for what their best instincts told them was the welfare of their neighbors and all mankind."

George Washington knew how much was enough and lived it for us all. We can live that way ourselves. We can all become *enoughers*.

What's at Stake?

In our personal lives as leaders, business owners and citizens, I feel this is a real and relevant question. I believe that intentionally answering the question of how much is enough has everything to do with our success and happiness. As the great poet, Adrienne Rich has said, "Poetry offers a way for people to hear their unspoken thoughts spoken." Now is our time …

Questions For Your Journal

1. What does this question, *how much is enough*, mean to you personally?

2. What conversation needs to happen now with your self and with others?

3. Where do you go from here?

AFTERWARD

Around the time of the final edits for this book, something serendipitous happened. I had an engaging and delightful conversation with a long-time friend and colleague who currently lives on a gorgeous island in the Pacific Northwest. Kevin Hoffberg and I go back very far. Twenty-five years far. I actually worked with Kevin in those days at one of the successful consulting ventures he had created.

Lucky for me, Kevin decided to reach out using that old-school telephone method to give me his feedback on the book. He had a number of helpful ideas, but one in particular was so simple, compelling and creative, that I just had to add it here in the afterward.

As stated in the book, I feel there is an unskillful dependence in our culture upon all things logical, strategic, empirical and linear. It's as though there had been a palace coup and the intuitive heart was forced to cede all control to the strategic mind. To again quote one of my mentors from afar, James March, Stanford Professor Emeritus: *"Leadership involves plumbing as well as poetry."*

Of course, nothing works right without skilled plumbing. However, something desperately human is lost when all we bring to the table are the rational, logical skills of a plumber. It is also folly to think we can bring only our inner-poet to the game of leadership. The goal is to blend and integrate the two. For example, why not let your *poet* decide the *why and what* to do, and then let your *plumber* carry out the *actual doing* in the smartest most rational way possible? Why indeed?

Well, of course this book has taken a solid stand for turning the heart and head into the kind of friends that naturally collaborate well together. Okay, so here is the point of this whole afterward. Kevin suggested that in addition to reading and enjoying great poetry, another way to plumb the depths of the heart and skillfully meld it with the mind is to begin a simple practice of journaling. As Kevin said (and I agree) journaling does not have to be a burdensome and formal activity. Just get a pen or pencil, buy a journal or notebook, and write. Yes, best to start tomorrow morning.

No, I mean it. Start tomorrow morning. Write a few lines of anything, a couple of insights, maybe two lines of poetry. Then carry them around for the rest of the day, and read them again at night. Once you've done that, write the next day and then the next. Carry your journal wherever you want, because after just a few days you'll be in it. Soon you will be hooked on writing for 10 to 30 minutes every day. You may find the practice to be more meditative and helpful than meditation itself. Or maybe you'll do both. Don't worry, just start.

In particular do not *try* to write. Do not try to be good or witty or clever. Do not think you should write at the level of *"War and Peace"* every time out. When you get stuck writing, just lower your standards and keep on going. The point is the *process* not the *product*. In fact, if you continue to restrain yourself from trying to be good, you may just find that your writing starts to *get* good.

Soon enough, you'll notice your heart giving up its core values, secrets and desires. And remember, there is no app for that, but rather something much better and more exciting. Just write and write every day.

Kevin and I realized during our conversation that we've both been journaling daily for years. We also realized that we both use the same brand of notebook. So please, get thyself to the keyboard, art store or fine stationary store, and order these items.

Item #1: Acquire a Moleskine notebook of whatever shape and size that attracts you. Kevin uses a smaller one he carries in his pocket. I use a fully stitched notebook size that goes in my satchel, although it stays in my office more than it travels.

> Note from their website: (us.moleskine.com) *"Moleskine was created as a brand in 1997, bringing back to life the legendary notebook used by artists and thinkers over the past two centuries: among them Vincent van Gogh, Pablo Picasso, Ernest Hemingway, and Bruce Chatwin."*

Item #2: Acquire a box of Blackwing 602 Pencils. Yes, I know I'm asking you to buy a dozen of the most expensive pencils you will ever buy. A dozen will set you back nearly two bucks a pencil. And yet, they are worth every penny in my humble opinion. I love my pencils so much I can't bear to throw them away. I have a whole box full of little Blackwing nubs so short that my fingers cramp trying to use them. Eventually they get so short, I give up using them, but never give them the toss.

> Note from their website: (blackwing602.com) *"Legendary Grammy, Emmy, Pulitzer and Academy*

Award winners have created with the Blackwing 602
pencil. The list of known users includes John Steinbeck,
Stephen Sondheim, Leonard Bernstein and Chuck Jones
who proudly used Blackwings to create Bugs Bunny and
many other Looney Tunes characters."

Remember: Please resist judging this practice until you've logged at least several months of daily writing. A year would be better. After that, write me and tell me what you've discovered about yourself and particularly your heart. If you are not thrilled with the practice, I will gladly purchase your remaining Blackwing 602 Pencils. And if you have extra Moleshine notebooks either Kevin or I will purchase those as well so long as you buy the kind we like. But trust me, I'm not concerned.

ABOUT THE AUTHOR

Dale Biron: Coach | Speaker | Author | Poet

Over the past 25 years Dale Biron has coached an extraordinary number of successful leaders and teams, fulfilling his mission to support clients in both their work and personal lives. Using bold, powerful language, he is transforming how timeless narratives and poems are experienced and applied.

Bucking tradition, Dale uses poetry in story-rich, entertaining and engaging ways that ignite the mind, unleash the imagination, and touch the heart and soul. He has long observed how great stories and poems integrate and draw out the best of our intellectual and emotional selves. Such poems and stories have wholehearted conversations built right in, making them exceptional tools for those who want to improve their communication and accomplish more together.

Dale has presented and taught at large and small venues throughout the West, including TEDx Marin, national business conferences, The Herbst Theatre, and Dominican University. He is former Poetry Editor for *A Network for Grateful Living* and served on the Board of Directors of the Marin Poetry Center. Dale's own book of poems—*Why We Do Our Daily Practice*—was published in 2014.

Growing up in the Piedmont region of North Carolina under the watchful care of a New England-bred Father who read voraciously and a Southern-born Mother who loved poetry, literature and Latin, Dale's love for language was predestined. He now lives, works and gardens in the beautiful San Francisco Bay Area.

Permissions

www.ingramcontent.com/pod-product-compliance
Lightning Source LLC
Chambersburg PA
CBHW031901090426
42741CB00005B/590